Doc at the Reference Desk

Small Stories in a Large Library

Thomas Mann

Alexandrina Press

Washington, D.C.

2017

PREFACE

These stories were written just for fun, to try to capture the feel of working at a reference desk in a very large library—but in an ideal fictional one where, among other concerns, you don't get fired for mouthing off. The Library of Congress, as represented here, is very much a fictional version of the real institution, where I spent some three decades without getting fired for offenses probably greater than any depicted here. Another motive behind these fictions is a wish to convey to potential future reference librarians some of the fun of being able to exploit "the tricks of the trade," about which most researchers haven't even the beginnings of a clue. I must add that, of course, the characters represented in these stories are creations of my imagination, not portraits of real people.

My thanks to all of the researchers I've helped over the decades, from whom I've learned more than I can convey.

CONTENTS

The Visit of the V.I.P

The guy wearing the "Distinguished Visitor" tag came into the reading room escorted by one of the administrative assistants from the Librarian's office. The badge from the Library, though, was conspicuously tucked behind another tag with "WHITE HOUSE VISITOR" in very big letters, with a third that had his new Executive Branch official picture for the whole world to see, well after he'd left the mansion. The LC assistant was Laura, who had worked her way up a few years ago from a career in Congressional Research Service, where I used to work with her.

He was wearing a $500 three-piece suit, was accompanied by a Mini-Me personal aide, and had his family in tow, too—a wife who walked carefully behind him along with a son and a daughter, college and high school age. The aide was short, with the skittish look of a rat caught in the open between holes. *Laura escorting a V.I.P. meant two things: the guy had enough money that the Librarian wanted him to get a favorable impression of the Library, but also that he didn't have enough dough for the Librarian himself to be bothered escorting him. Probably some honcho who figured he could buy some prestige for himself by donating enough to get on the Council—a.k.a. the Librarian's Club—but not important enough to raise the Library's own image. Candidates for that group got the Librarian as tour guide.*

Laura was starting her tour spiel. "This is the Main Reading Room, where most researchers start. We actually have twenty other reading rooms, but of course none of the others look like this." And gesturing to my counter she started to say, "And this is where you talk to the reference librarians, who will help you find the books—"

"Oh, *books*," the guy laughed, looking around at his entourage for approval. He got it from the rat. "As I was telling the President this morning, where I'm Dean we just put up a hundred million dollar Engineering complex, and all of my professors in the department said they didn't want any space at all set aside for a library—it's all online now."

Mini-me jumped in to let me know that "Dr. Teufelsdrockh is an informal advisor to the President on education matters." This clarification, however, was met with a stern glare of disapproval from his boss, who immediately corrected him with the apparently correct term "unpaid advisor" rather than the lesser "informal." The mistake was as bad, in Washington terms, as confusing a Deputy Assistant Director and an Assistant Deputy Director.

The great man continued. "In my school every office and cubicle has electronic access to everything everybody needs. My professors said the only paper they wanted was in the washrooms!" He and his aide laughed again. Mr. V.I.P. evidently took great pride in owning so many smart people. The little aide stood with his hands clasped behind his back, the way the British Royals do; I figured he'd been trained that way with morsels of cheese for reinforcement. He kept his eyes on the boss's face; after his previous *faux pas* he was now more than ever intent on matching exactly whatever mood showed up there. Laura was eyeing me in just the same way— not to copy what I showed, but in practiced readiness to steer certain kinds of visitors quickly past me. She was about to get more practice.

The Eminence turned to his kids. "Come on in--I want you to see what libraries used to be, when they still had books. They do *look* pretty good—I'll go that far." He smiled paternally, to show us all that his pragmatic, no-nonsense business mind still retained something of a nostalgic and sentimental side. Then he turned to me. I was looking him over at the same time. *On those $500 lapels surrounding his prominent credentials he had a Phi Beta Kappa pin, a little American flag, and another pin you could buy for yourself when you get listed in* Who's Who. *His tie had the name of a California university spelled out in letters formed to look like microchip circuits, and one of his three rings was big enough to put a Super Bowl winner's to shame. The last time I'd seen hair dyed as dark brown as his was at a funeral parlor, on the guest of honor; but no undertaker would've bothered with the expense of a comparable cap job on the teeth.*

"So you're a *reference librarian*." He said it like he'd hooked a coelacanth on an exotic fishing vacation. "What do you actually *do*, now that everything's online and people can find it all on Google and Wikipedia? These days, isn't that like being a door-to-door encyclopedia salesman?" He laughed at his own little joke. Mini-Me chuckled out loud.

I smiled too. Laura held her breath. "Well, I guess you must live so far out West that our Pony Express riders haven't reached you with the news yet, that us East Coasters still haven't repealed the Copyright law. That might have something to do with the fact that back here we're still adding over twelve hundred volumes to the collection every day. Would you believe it?—actual bound, printed, physical *books* that nobody's digitized because it happens to be illegal. And—even harder to believe—that includes over 10,000 specialized *encyclopedias* that have been published just in the last decade. I know it strains credibility, but they actually cover lots of things that aren't in Wikipedia—and to judge by their sheer proliferation, whoever's selling all those thousands of sets must be making a pile of money, even without the door-to-door sales people. But then I guess all of your pet geniuses in their cubicle mazes don't need any of those millions of undigitized pages to keep themselves just as smart as you are."

Laura was now figuring how to keep her own job.

The rat didn't know how to copy the look the guy gave me, so he just froze. The two kids were wide-eyed. Mr. Important cleared his throat and forced another laugh. At this point his gaze shifted above my head, as though looking for anyone more important than me to talk to. "But don't you think," he said, addressing the top of the wall and fingering his White House talisman, "that all of those copyright bumps will be *worked out*, so even the current books will all be freely available online? Isn't it a matter of keeping up with the inevitable evolution, to stay on the right side of history? My kids get all they need right now from their Kindles and tablets—we don't even keep books in the

4

house."

The daughter—the high school age one—piped up at that. "But we *would*, Daddy, if you'd let us! Those Jane Austen novels that Aunt Stephanie gave me—"

Her mother—a nice looking plump woman but, I figured, hovering somewhere in the "holding" status of pre-Trophy Wife—shushed her immediately while turning a deeper shade of red herself.

"Oh, I understand completely," I said. "We're running out of space ourselves to hold all of the paper stuff that isn't free on the Internet. In fact, right up in the balcony of Alcove 4, just around the corner, we've got a full hardcopy set of the *U.S. Code*—that's the annoying set with the big Title 17 volume on Copyright law. Come to think of it, since there *is* an online version of it, maybe you could do us a favor and take the printed set off our hands? I mean, you said it yourself—those engineers of yours still need some real paper in those new washrooms, don't they? Or have they done that inevitable evolution thing so far in advance of the rest of us that now they just download ones and zeroes instead of crapping—so their cracks just need to be swiped instead of wiped?"

The kids broke out laughing. Even the rat had to stifle himself, which I figured did not bode well for his own continued employment. Mr. Big, whose view over my head had still not turned up any substitute interlocutor recognizably as important as himself, seemed somewhat at a loss for words, as though one of his pet mice had actually said something out loud.

But then Laura jumped in, probably to save everybody's job. "Well, Doc *is* known for his sense of humor around here." She curled her arm in the V.I.P.'s. "But come over here—you still have to see the Reading Room! It's really magnificent!" She ushered Mr. *Who's Who* and the little guy off into the Room; but the wife held the kids back.

She shrugged her shoulders while nodding towards the husband's back—a gesture that looked well practiced. Then she said to the kids, "Go ahead and ask—you won't have the opportunity to use a library like this when we get home."

The boy was kind of shy about asking for help, but looking out at his Dad going into the Reading Room with Laura, he did seem to realize he had an opportunity with a time limit on it. "Something came up in one of my classes last week. One of the readings made a reference to a Nazi group that was trying to re-write the Bible to take out the parts they objected to. Nobody could find what the organization was. Our prof said he'd give extra credit to anybody who could identify it."

I liked this kid. He didn't ask, "Where are the books on Germany?"—he asked for exactly what he wanted to find. A good first step—and a very unusual one, these days. This kid knew how to start a project.

"C'mon over here," I said. Something like that is likely to be in the DD area—that's where we have reference books on German history. I walked all three of them over to the alcove just around the corner, and looked at a half-dozen shelves of DDs. What especially caught my eye was a two-volume set, *Encyclopedia of Nazi Germany*. I didn't even know we had such a thing, but the subject-shelving brought it to my attention. I gave the kid the first volume and told him to look under "Bible" while I looked in the index at the back of volume 2. It had a cross-reference from "Old Testament" to "Species-true Christianity." "Here," I said, "Take a look at this."

The kid devoured the article; it gave a cross-reference to any even longer entry on "League for a German Church." "It's here!' he said to his Mom. It was something called *Bund für Deutsche Kirk*; it wanted to get rid of the Jewish Old Testament." He turned to me. "Do you mind if I take a picture of this?" He had his smartphone out already. I told him to go right ahead. "I don't think we'll have this back home at Dad's university—they sent most of the books out to a warehouse."

At that point the wife prodded the little girl, who didn't need much prodding. "What *I* need is something about a Russian ballerina. She paid a lot of famous composers to write things for her."

"You have her name?"

She took a little notebook out of her purse. The cover had the famous silhouette of Jane Austen on it. *I like this kid, too*, I thought— *she has penciled notes in it, with inflated upper loops, and little smiling flowers drawn in the margins. She actually knows cursive handwriting. Mom's attention, I bet. Certainly not Dad's.*

"It's Ida Rubinstein," she said, pointing to the last name, "and 'Rubinstein' is spelled with an 'i'." That last detail told me she'd asked for help before. But apparently didn't get what she needed.

"Let's try over here in the Gs." *As with her brother's question, there wouldn't be time to turn in any call slips—it'd have to be an encyclopedia right at hand.* "Here—*The International Encyclopedia of Dance*. . . Looks like a three-page article on her."

"It's got a picture that's not the same as the ones in Wikipedia!" she exclaimed to her Mom, "and this is longer, too, with more sources at the end!" She looked at her brother, who already had his camera phone ready. She held the book while he clicked over it. "Don't forget the title page," he said, "You'll need to show where you got the copy." *Yeah. This kid would do all right.*

I could see Laura out in the reading room gesturing up to the statues and the ceiling. From where she was pointing I could tell she was half-way through her tour.

Then the wife piped up. "I wonder if *I* can ask something?"

"Same price for everything."

"You probably don't have this right at your fingertips, but my sister is trying to do our genealogy, and she's been looking for a photograph of an ancestor. He was some kind of big manufacturer in the 1920s."

"If you've got his name we can try right over here." I walked them over to the old *National Cyclopaedia of American Biography*. "This has a lot of write-ups and pictures of businessmen from that period who didn't make it into the regular *Who's Who* books."

She took a quick look in the Index volume I pulled down for her, then zeroed in on one of the big green volumes. "Here he is!—a nice article and a full-page photograph! Stephanie will love this!"

"Well, I guess you'll all have something real to show when you get back, other than just a few postcards of the place."

The son was busy texting something. A second later he looked up. "I don't have to wait to get back. I just sent my prof that article on the *Bund*. And I just found an article on it in Wikipedia, too—it's there but nobody in class found it because we couldn't figure out which words to type in. That German name did it!" He trained his smartphone on the *National Cyclopaedia* article. "Mom, if you have Aunt Stephanie's email we can send her this right away, too."

At that moment, though, I could see Laura was headed back to the reference desk area with Mr. Distinguished. Wife, kids, and I were closer so we got there first. Laura had earned her keep by talking continually about the history of the building as she steered the guy and the rat right past me. Neither one gave me even a glance.

They moved into the cross-corridor, where I couldn't overhear everything that was being said; but evidently the V.I.P. was surprised by the three big smiles he was surrounded with. I caught a couple snatches of three different voices, though: " . . . those homework assignments you tried to help with" . . . "Daddy, can we get that *Dance* encyclopedia!?" . . . "found everything *all in ten minutes*" . . . . "didn't even look at a computer, Dad!" . . . "everything was in *books!*"

Somebody else came up to the reference desk just then, wanting information on the folklore of pig-killing in Hungary; that kept me busy for a few minutes, and then there was somebody else. And somebody else after that—the usual. I forgot all about Mr. V.I.P.

Until about a week later. I got a holey envelope in inter-office mail. It was from Laura. She had attached a little unsigned note in a handwriting I recognized.

It read, simply, "Thanks. Some donors just aren't worth the upkeep."

Prospero's Island

Middle-aged man. Hurrying past the reference desk, heading directly into the reading room—haven't seen him before—evidently not going to ask any questions. Blue sport coat, brown tie, plaid sport shirt, khaki slacks, large plastic '90s eyeglass frames, tan ankle boots—your basic academic clash. Might've got up early and dressed in the dark. No—turning on light wouldn't have helped. Single—no wife to tell him. Suntanned—outdoors. Carrying a book—one word title decipherable on the fly: "Nabokov." Outdoors and academic. Nabokov. Butterflies.

As he headed into the reading room I searched the online catalog under "Nabokov" expecting to see the "—Bibliography" subdivision under it. It was there, a 214 page volume—then I switched to *Web of Science* to check for any recent literature review overview articles on butterflies. *Academics don't find bibliographies. Know even less about literature review articles.* Several on wing and eyespot patterns, one on the history of classification, two others with more than 200 footnotes apiece.

While I made the printout a young girl came up.

Ohio State sweatshirt. Way too large—boyfriend gift. No wedding ring. No boyfriend with her. Probably in town for the holiday, back to see family.

"Where do I turn in these call slips?"

"At the central desk there, but first you have to write in a desk number where the books will be delivered. Or your last name if you don't want to wait—it takes about an hour. You could go have lunch and the books would be waiting for you when you get back."

"An *hour?*" *Always used to open stacks and no waiting.*

"Yeah. But I can show you some databases you can be looking at in the meantime. What are you working on—what's the project?"

"Well, some of these articles my boyfriend wants me to get for him. He couldn't find them at school, but I told him I'd check the Library of Congress while I'm back here. I'm also working on my Master's thesis."

"Good. You may not know it, but we have a full set of American doctoral dissertations here. There's a couple million of 'em, and they don't show up in the book catalog. You have to search *Dissertations and Theses*—it's a separate database, and it's not on the open Internet. You can't read all of those dissertations for free anywhere else. What's your topic?"

"Oh, it's on Proust. But that's a good idea. I should try dissertations."

"Well, we've got a ton of stuff on Proust, beyond just dissertations. "Y'know, within that, what are you ultimately doing?"

It's a study of Bergson's influence on him. I've already done the *MLA Bibliography*. But I'm not finding any recent articles."

"Okay, but the older stuff may be just as good as the recent for something like that."

"Yeah. That's right. But is the older material online?"

The usual: 'if it's not online it doesn't exist.'

"Probably not, but you can still find it through bibliographies; and we'll still have it in paper copies. You may not be able to get those at all at your home library." I motioned her around the desk. Here, look at the screen." In the regular book catalog I quickly found 500-page bibliographies on both Proust and Bergson. Before making printouts I cleared the Nabokov printouts from the hopper.

"If you look in the index to the *Proust* bibliography for 'Bergson,' and in the *Bergson* bibliography for 'Proust,' you can cover the older literature pretty well. It's a way of doing combinations without a computer, for stuff not in the databases. Bibliographies compiled by scholars are usually much better than printouts; but you want to use both."

"I've already done *JSTOR* for the old articles."

"Well, keep in mind that *JSTOR* includes only about 2,000 journals. The Library of Congress has well over 100,000 electronic journals, and maybe 300,000 in paper and microfilm. *JSTOR* is fine, but it's not even close to covering everything relevant. You might also try a few other databases." I made a list of a half-dozen, some full-text, and explained what they cover. "But let me show you some literature criticism sets we have right out in the reading room. You can be looking at them while the books are being fetched." *Always 'online'—they won't look at paper unless you put it right in front of 'em. But then they really will.*

As I led her over to the alcove we passed Nabokov-man. He'd just left his notebook and laptop at a desk, first row on the right, to turn in call slips at the central station. They were telling him he needs to go to the Microforms room for one of the call numbers. His back was to us. I left the bibliography printout and butterfly overview articles on his desk as I walked by.

Back at the reference desk, it was the hour, and time to switch over to the station in the computer room. Fifty-eight terminals, with three-quarters being used. Pretty busy. Half doing the catalog; the other half split among subscription databases, open websites, and email. One guy with his own earphones, chuckling to himself over some video.

One of the searchers was looking at the *Dissertations* file. *Good. Been here before, probably many times, and eventually had that pointed out. They never find it on their own. Now she knows to check it. Something about 'memsahibs' on her screen.*

Middle-aged. Small rimless glasses on a chain—more concerned about her appearance than the butterfly guy. This time of day in the middle of the week just after Christmas, looking for dissertations, gotta be another academic. In town for the MLA conference, playing hooky like the Nabokov-guy and spending the day at the Library. Good—better here than what they'd get at the convention. Lapel pin with elephant and howdah. Silver, handmade. India. Been there herself. Feminist slant. English or History. Maybe Anthropology. No—gotta be English: the convention.

At the reference station I quickly searched for "memsahib*" in *Periodicals Contents Index, Nineteenth Century Masterfile, Historical Abstracts*—dozens of citations, and then a few full text articles in *Gerritsen* database for women's studies. I printed them all.

Then Nabokov-man wandered back to the computers; as he walked past the memsahib-lady she called out to him.

"John! Hello! Getting in some research, I see—make hay while the sun shines!"

"Claire! Well, hello yourself! I was hoping I'd run into you!" They hug. "I see you have the same idea—I do like being in Florida, but it *doesn't* have the Library of Congress. And I couldn't sit through one more minute of 'Transgressive Alterity in *Lolita*,' so here I am. What's your excuse?"

She told him. Both at the convention. Exchanged hotel information. Asked how colleagues are doing.

"Seriously: you really should visit Florida sometime. This year we have quite a colony of Monarch butterflies with us, you know. It's really a sight. Not all of them go to Mexico."

He asked her about lunch.

She smiled. "We can go to the cafeteria in the Madison Building—I've been there before. The food's pretty good. I just have to stay away from the pay-by-weight section—I have to keep inside my 'academic expense account'!" They both laughed. "But the cafeteria doesn't open for the public for another twenty minutes—12:30. How about if we meet then—I'm at desk 32 in the reading room." Bargain struck.

And desk number for memsahib printouts. Would be good to check the Z7900s too—the women's bibliographies, nowhere near whatever "D" history classes may have "memsahibs." I wandered out into the reference collection Zs. *Here: 1049 pages in* 200 Years of British Women Autobiographies. *Next shelf,* Women in English Social History 1800-1914 *with third volume on autobiographies. And* Women in the British Empire: An Annotated Guide to Sources. *Bingo. Desk 32.*

I was back at the computer station, twenty minutes later. Nabokov and memsahib were on their way out of the reading room, gesturing to the librarian at the desk across the hall. Asked if she knew how the printouts and bibliographies showed up at both their desks. Librarian didn't have a clue.

"But this is amazing. I didn't even order these things, and neither did she. They were just *there*, at our desks!" The librarian shrugged, said she's glad they're happy, whatever the reason. They passed to the corridor.

"They *can't* be monitoring what we do at the computers," he says.

"I made my printouts back in Gainesville, from their web page, so I'd have the call numbers ready as soon as I got here. I didn't even touch a keyboard until after I ran into you! And it takes an hour for books to be delivered, and you hadn't even turned in *any* of your call slips yet. Those were great bibliographies and we didn't even ask for them! And the printouts came from databases we didn't even know about! How does this place work? Is it *magic*?"

I kept a straight face as they walked by. Pretended not to notice. *"Thy shape invisible retain thou still."* Yeah. Magic. *Try finding that on the Internet.*

Without a Compass

Two kids made it past the security guard at 8:50 that morning—showed their new library I.D.s, signed in, and came up to the reference desk. It had been a quiet morning—no readers at all 'til then—leaving time just to look up at the ceiling. Plaster goddesses of the different areas of knowledge—History, Poetry, Religion, Law—looked down, half smiling, maybe half crying at the uses to which the passing ants below scurried to employ them. How many of those uses would wind up in still more books, jostling their millions of brethren already in the crowded shelves; how many more would just answer some little question of the moment, with problem and ant both vanishing together. I thought of all the dissertations on Madonna and Buffy the Vampire Slayer. Still, maybe one connection, one in a thousand, would open up a new channel, light a fire, change a life. *"The readiness is all."*

The girl spoke up first. "Hi—we're *totally* lost. This is our first time here."

The guy added, somewhat sheepishly, "I've lived in this area most of my life and I've never been here either."

"Well, it's about time you got here. We got 25 million books, and you've just been goofing off with the Internet the whole semester.

Okay, you're here now, and that's the important thing." They both laughed. "What's your project?" *Ask* them *what they're researching and they won't be shy. You won't have to pry out what they really want.*

"We're actually doing separate things. Hers is for school, so that's more important." He looked at her. "You go first."

I made a quick scan; everything raced through. *Both college age, undergrad, both in jeans; the girl wearing a Northwestern U. sweatshirt. Both with Mac laptops. The guy in ankle-high boots, well worn—a big scuff on one side. Not the kind of wear you get from just walking around Evanston. Knees worn, too. Carabineer hanging from his belt loop, with nothing attached. Probably a water bottle he had to check in the cloakroom. Okay, hardcore camper, rock climber, something like that. The girl—that N.U. sweatshirt too big for her. Probably the guy's—yeah, his girlfriend. Carrying some heavy book in the clear plastic bag they were issued in the checkroom—too big for a basic trade book. Hardcover, no jacket, casewrap binding—some kind of color photo image on the cover. Gotta be a textbook—no dust jacket—can't see the title, but thick enough for an Intro or survey course. Maybe History? Or Art? If it were science or business they'd've been directed to the other building when they got their I.D.s. Her necklace, though—one of those little Declaration of Independence repros they sell at the Archives. Go with History. Both in town for the long Memorial Day weekend—day one already spent at the museums. Conspicuous DC history souvenir. You don't see that on the natives—so she must be from out of town, visiting him, the local guy—maybe getting introduced to his family for the first time? This must be their second free day in DC—see the sites on day one, do some term paper research at the Library on day two. And they're here twenty minutes after opening time—just enough for them to get their LC I.D.s and check their backpacks. Planned this trip carefully in advance.*

"Well, I have to write a paper on Millard Fillmore's foreign policy; they told me at the registration to come here first, but I'm not sure if I should be here or in the Manuscripts department. I'm supposed to include at least two primary sources, and I have no idea where to begin." She gestured to her boyfriend. "He's doing something on his own."

"I guess so. I'm interested in navigation. Sort of."

"Not ships' navigation on the ocean, but like hikers' navigation in the woods?"

"Yeah, like that!"

"Okay—do you mean like 'orienteering,' or doing those treasure hunts with GPS locators?"

"No. I've done those! This is different. It's more like when there are people in deserts or mountains, when they got lost they could still figure out where they were even without GPS. Just from seeing things in their surroundings. It's sort of like trackers who can notice things on the ground that everybody else would miss. That kind of thing. But it's not orienteering—that has a compass. And it's not tracking, exactly. I didn't find much on Google—there's no good word for it. There were a few websites, but they were pretty superficial. I'm curious to see if there's a whole book on it."

"Okay, that's do-able. One thing, though—this is a closed-stacks library, so you can't just go into the bookstacks and browse around yourself; you have to identify what you want through the computer and some other things I can show you, then fill out call slips. It takes about forty-five minutes for delivery, so maybe we should get some Fillmore stuff in the pipeline first; then we can do the navigating. Would that be okay?"

They nodded. To the girl: "How long does your paper have to be?"

"Under fifteen pages, but probably over ten would be best. I found some short things in Google and Wikipedia about Fillmore opening up Japan; but everybody else will be using that, and I need a good grade on this, so if I can come up with something original that would be ideal. But I am *totally* overwhelmed by this place."

"Well, this is the place you want to be—come on back here and let me show you a few things to start with."

I led them into the Main Reading Room, slowing down appreciably when we crossed the threshold—when the sight of the 160' dome, the Kentucky and Algerian marble, and all those goddesses is new, it's best to allow a moment or two for the inevitable "Wow!" reaction. It came.

"Yeah, they don't build 'em like this anymore," I said. "What you're seeing here, though, apart from the architecture, is just the reference collection—about 60,000 volumes around the circle.

Anything in here, you can help yourself to, including the first balcony level. You don't need to turn in call slips. But remember this is 60,000 out of 25 *million*—most of it's in closed stacks."

"Isn't this where they filmed *National Treasure*?" the girl almost squealed.

"Most of the filming was up at the top level, over there. But right here is the door Nicolas Cage went through to get up there."

I led them into Deck 7, off the reading room, where the reference collection continues with the later letters in the classification scheme— Q through Z, that don't fit in the circle.

"We may not find a book with the key to a lost city of gold back here, but I suspect we will find one with the Secrets of Millard Fillmore towards the back. Fortunately, we don't get a lot of conspiracy theorists hounding us on that particular subject. I think you may have a clear field there, without much competition."

"Yeah, I don't suppose you get many questions about Millard Fillmore." The guy smirked and gave the girl a nudge with his elbow. She elbowed him back just as hard.

"Actually, you'd be surprised," I said. We had a White House researcher here for a year and a half, reconstructing his book collection. Fillmore and his wife were the first to create an official White House library. You'd be surprised what people are working on. Even the really obscure stuff gets used."

I led them straight back to the very end, to the Z8000s. Of course, there was a book-length bibliography on Millard Fillmore. It had a forty page section listing over 300 sources on Fillmore's foreign policy in relation to dozens of countries—way beyond Japan.

"You want to look through this to start—it'll give you a good overview of what's available across the board. It may also identify some primary sources right there. But we're not done—come on over here." I walked back a few aisles, got myself oriented, and picked out a hefty two-volume set dated 2003, *American Foreign Relations since 1600: A Guide to the Literature.* I had never seen it before. "Here—look under 'Fillmore' in the Index—this may open it up a little more."

The guy looked at me with evident interest. "Do you know every book in this whole collection?"

"No, not individual titles. But I generally know where groups of things are likely to be. I have a few markers to steer by. Subject bibliographies always have Z call numbers, so that's why we're starting off back here, at the end of the sequence. If you can find an annotated bibliography compiled by a scholar, it's usually a better starting point than any computer printout. Within the Zs, bibliographies on individual people, like Presidents or literary figures, are always in the last row, in the Z8000s, if you want to get technical about it. Within that area they're just arranged by the last name of the people the bibliographies are about. I figured there oughta be one on Fillmore just because there are bibliographies done on most Presidents; and if there *is* one, that's where it should be. And that's where it was.

"With the 'foreign relations' I was looking over here in a different sequence. There's actually an alphabetical arrangement to this part of the bibliography collection. The 'International relations' group, for shelving purposes, is a subset of the 'L' for 'Law' area; and 'L' follows 'J' for 'Jewish studies' pretty closely. I use this shelf of Holocaust books as an alphabetical signpost for the 'J's since people are always doing research on that. Any good sources on 'L' subjects should be shelved right nearby, even though the title on this set says 'Foreign Relations' rather than 'Law'. You have to go by the alphabetical category the catalogers use, even if it's not the one that shows up in the actual titles. You can see the sequence if you know it's there, but it's not something that leaps out at you if you're not a librarian. I didn't know about this specific set; I just knew what area books like that ought to be in. But we're not done yet. Come on out here."

I took them out into the Main Reading Room, up one of the winding stairways to the balcony of Alcove 2. "You might take a look through this *Annals of America* set; it's 22 volumes of primary sources on American history. And look around a bit in this same area—the 'E' class numbers here are all on American history. In fact, here's a new encyclopedia, *U.S. Presidents' Foreign Policies from 1789 to the Present*, with, let's see, a five page article on Fillmore, with recommended sources at the end. Not bad for an initial overview."

Her eyes almost popped. *Probably not used to using a real library. With actual books. Sometimes, these days, they don't even know what a call number is.*

"But then you want to check something in the next balcony over, too." We went single-file over to Alcove 3—the walkway in the balconies is pretty narrow; but I could see out of the corner of my eye how overwhelmed the kids still were, just from the architecture. And now they were even more into it—physically into it, walking around the actual passages and seeing where the real treasures were hidden. "Here—you want to look at this set of *Messages and Papers of the Presidents*—with this, and that *Annals* set, you may have your two primary sources right there. But then that encyclopedia article and those bibliographies will probably tell you about others. You'll have to turn in call slips for whatever sources they list; but when you get to that point, show me, or any of the other librarians, whichever citations look good, and we can show you how to do it."

The guy was giving me that interested look again. I tapped on the spine of the *Messages and Papers* set—"J81. Yeah, the low 'J' numbers mean something too. I don't know what '81' refers to, but I know this is the classification area for Presidential Papers, in relation to some other 'political' sources shelved around here; 'J' as a class number means something different from 'J' as an alphabetical marker in the bibliographies downstairs. Just knowing what's generally in the area was enough to get me here. I didn't remember this particular title, but I knew the set, whatever you call it, would be somewhere around in this class area."

"One other thing," I told the girl, "we have some databases that have digitized full texts of several hundred American newspapers from the 19th century, and other databases with thousands of digitized periodicals from the same period. Contemporary write-ups like that might also count as primary sources—but it's not a good idea to just jump into huge full-text databases until you've got a lot clearer idea of what you're looking for."

"Yeah!" She half-nodded, half shook her head. "I tried Google Books and Google Scholar back at school and I just couldn't wade through everything. I think this encyclopedia and these bibliographies should help a lot!"

I suggested that she pick out a desk in the reading room and start looking through the sources she already had, and maybe browse the "E" reference area a bit more on her own, while I took the guy with me back to the desk.

"Here's something else you want to show your girlfriend." I pulled out a volume of the *Encyclopedia of U. S. Foreign Relations* set, shelved right nearby the reference desk, and quickly found an article on "Fillmore" within it. "This is another little overview article on his foreign policy, with a brief listing of highly-recommended readings at the end. One of them—here—*The Cambridge History of American Foreign Relations*, might be especially worth a look. Why don't you take this out to her, and get set up with your laptops—there are plugs underneath the desks if you need them—and then come back. I'm gonna try something else while you do that."

"Yeah—this is great! I'll be back!" I could almost see the wheels turning in his head: girlfriend gets 'A' paper in History class because boyfriend took her to Library of Congress. Girlfriend is *grateful* to boyfriend . . .

While he was gone I took a quick look in *America: History and Life* and *Dissertations and Theses,* to see if anything particularly good came up about Fillmore and foreign relations; but nothing leapt out at me, so I thought I'd hold off mentioning either database. They might still be of use later, along with *Nineteenth Century Masterfile* and a couple others, once the girl had focused her topic a bit more.

Five minutes later the guy was back, to ask about his own interest.

"Do you have any good sources on it already, or any good example of it?" *At least the kid's comfortable now—he's asking for what he really wants, not just 'navigation' in general. I wonder if that's all he typed into Google.*

"Yeah, actually. I got the idea from a book I read about Timbuktu, in Africa. It had a few pages on an old Saharan guide; he was famous for leading people through the desert. It had some stories about how he could figure out where he was, in the middle of nowhere, just by observing things about the soil, or features on the horizon. He once rescued an army patrol over a walkie-talkie—they were lost in the desert but he had them describe their surroundings to him, and the appearance of the sand. That's all he needed to figure out where they were. He was pretty shrewd, too—he wouldn't tell them how to get back until they agreed to give him a raise."

"Okay, but the whole book isn't on what he did, right?—it's just a few pages?

"Yeah. What I'd really like would be to *find* a whole book on how he did it."

I turned to the red book set that lists all of the Library of Congress Subject Headings. I thought I'd try "Orienteering" even though that wasn't exactly what the kid wanted; the starting point didn't matter, as long as it was somewhere in the ballpark—once you get into the cross-reference network, you can move around among the subject terms pretty efficiently even if you know nothing about the topic. The system is set up to show you what you don't know how to ask for exactly. What caught my eye right away was the heading "Orientation," right near "Orienteering." I thought I'd try that in the catalog as an initial stab, to see what kind of results it would bring up.

Right on the first screen a good citation showed up: *Finding Your Way Without Map or Compass*, by a Harold Gatty. The catalog record for it provided two other headings: "Wilderness survival" and "Navigation." I suggested to the kid that he turn in a call slip for the Gatty book right away, to get it in the pipeline; then try all three of the LC headings himself back in the computer catalog area—his eyeball would be better than mine in sifting the results.

I showed him where to turn in his call slip, and went back to the reference desk. Another kid was there, wanting stuff on examples of early "globalization" in eighteenth century U.S. trade practices; and he was followed by somebody doing a project on quartermasters in the army in World War II; and then a grad student who wanted to know how visitors behave in zoos; and somebody else working on a biography of a Congressman who was his great-grandfather. Those took up the rest of the morning.

I was back after lunch, and the 'navigation' kid walked by again, on his way to the computers. He was all lit up.

That Gatty book is *perfect*—it's exactly the kind of thing I wanted. I'd never heard of him, but the book gives some information about him—he was the best navigator in the world back in the '30s and '40s, and he learned it all before computers. He really *studied* things like land forms and tree shapes and wave patterns in the ocean—this whole thing was his life's passion! He knew all about deserts and forests and polar regions and stars and even sea birds! I never knew this book existed; but I'm gonna get on Amazon right now and order a copy for myself!"

"Well, good." I felt like an old codger, but I said it anyway: "Sometimes the older books do have the best information. There probably aren't too many people with that kind of pre-GPS experience writing today."

"Not many, no; but those subject headings you found did turn up some recent books too, that look very good. I ordered them too." Then he gave me that look again. "You were doing that yourself, inside. That whole reference collection—what did you say it was, 60,000 volumes?—it's just a huge wilderness to me; but you could spot markers in it, all over, that mean something, that the rest of us don't see. You could tell how to get to all the right places without even looking at a computer. I know some of Shari's friends that are in her same class, and they've wasted whole days wading through Internet stuff—and you found more in fifteen minutes, without even looking at a screen. It's like there's this huge forest of books that makes no sense to anybody else looking at it; but you saw all sorts of pathways in it that took you right where you wanted to go. That's pretty amazing. I may want to learn how to do *that* after I figure out the land navigation tricks!"

"Well, it comes in handy," I said. "And we could always use a few more good reference librarians. But I have a question for you. That Saharan guide you mentioned—did he get his raise?

"Yeah, he did."

"Good for him. I could use a raise myself."

Still the Same Old Story

"Is this where I turn in these call slips?"

Cashmere sweater and short skirt, on a very cold afternoon in January. Not your basic sweatshirt and jeans. Long hair worn straight down, not tied up. Meeting a guy here later; or right after she leaves the library.

I looked at the slips to see if she'd written in a desk number or her last name. *Three books on the movie Casablanca. Old enough to be a grad student. Thesis? Dissertation?*

"You want to write down either a desk number where you're sitting, here; or your last name, and turn in the slips at the Center Desk. It takes about forty-five minutes. If you write your name you can be doing more searches, or go have a coffee in the meantime, and the books'll be waiting at the Center Desk when you get back." *Always ask.* "What are you working on?"

"Oh, it's a paper for a course on screenwriting, on how Hollywood movies used stage scripts, and how they changed them."

"Hold on a second. Let me try something on the computer here." *The literature people never search the history databases. America:*

History and Life. Boolean 'Films and Drama.' Casablanca. Here—take a look."

Among the hits were three good ones:

"Time Goes By: A Casablanca Chronology." 114 events from 1923-99.

"Nobody Ever Loved Me That Much: A Casablanca Bibliography." 162 entries.

"The American Film Theater: An Examination of the Process of Adaptation from Stage to Screen in Theory and Practice." A dissertation.

"Let's see," she said. "I've got the first two—they were in the *MLA*. And I did Google searches too. But that third one looks fantastic! How did you do that?" As she'd stepped around to see the terminal I could see the cover of her notebook. *One of the U. of California campuses.*

"Well, you know not everything's on the Internet; and the *MLA* database can be pretty spotty. We'll have that dissertation here—you just need the UMI order number; that's the call number we use in the Microforms Room." *Draw out the question.* "Are you concentrating on *Casablanca* specifically?"

"Not really; it's more general than that, although I'm using it as one of my examples of how stage plays got run through the studio system. Maybe I should ask you, though. The librarians at my school couldn't come up with something related: I'd really like to see the original script of *Casablanca* as it was written for the stage, before the studio got hold of it. I was told to try WorldCat, but it's not in there. Actually, it is listed; but no library locations are given. The only locations are for a revised version of the script, not for the original. It's pretty weird."

"The original title was different, wasn't it—'Everybody Comes to Rick's,' or something like that?"

"That's it exactly!"

"Do you have the author?"

"Yeah—it's Murray Burnett, with two 't's.""

"You should look for that name in the old *Pre-56 National Union Catalog*."

"Is that a big green set? The librarian at my school told me not to bother with it, that everything in there was in WorldCat. I had asked about it when WorldCat didn't provide a location, because one of my teachers had mentioned it in my Methods class. But even he said it was a 'dinosaur'; and the library had sent the whole set to remote storage. Besides, somebody told me that whole green set now *is* online. But I didn't bother to check that if it's all in WorldCat anyway."

"We have the set right off Alcove 3. Try it. I bet it'll work. My experience is that there's a lot of stuff in there that WorldCat doesn't have. There were even a couple studies done on it—about 30% of the entries in the *NUC* aren't in the database." The online version is in HathiTrust, which is sort of like Google Books; but it's a very clunky search software—you can't keyword-search the whole thing all at once. And you have to do a lot of scrolling through print that's very tiny on a screen. Check the books—it's much easier and much faster."

I showed her on the map of the reading room where the set was shelved, and explained to her where to go for the dissertation that had turned up. She went off towards the *NUC*.

A young guy came up just as she left. *Hewlett Packard PC in the plastic carrying bag we give them when they have to check their backpacks. Probably a student. Right age for some Congressional staffers, though; but they never come in with laptops. If he asks about free photocopying first, though, he's a staffer.*

"You may not remember me, but you helped me a lot last semester. You untangled a pretty garbled citation I had. Right now I'm just trying to find a library in the area that has a couple rare books. You don't have them here."

"What's your project?

"I'm trying to compare all of the 18th century printings of a particular book. You've got copies from 1783 and 1785, but I also need to look at 1796 and 1798 impressions. They're not in your Rare Book room, or in your catalog. Here—let me get it exactly: it's *The Advantages and Disadvantages of the Married State*—it goes on from there with one of those long 18th century titles that fills up the whole page. But the author's name is John Johnson."

"Is it American? Or British?

"American."

"We may have the copies you want anyway, even if they're not in the catalog. They could be in a couple full-text databases—maybe Google Books or HathiTrust—or in microfilm collections. Would copies like that be okay, or do you need to look at things like bindings and watermarks?"

"Just the texts would be fine for what I need. I hadn't thought of Google or Hathi. I *will* need a good photocopy of at least the title page, and some of the Google stuff I've seen before is kind of fuzzy. I'll try that, but if you've got some other database or microfilm I'd like to know about it."

"Let's try Google Books right here." I called up the Advanced Search page and typed in the title. Seven listings, but none full-text. "Okay, no luck there, but we're not done." I took a quick look in *Early American Imprints*, and, sure enough, there was a full-text of the 1796 edition copy—and a 1794 that he hadn't been aware of.

"Let me set you up on one of the public terminals, across the hall—that way you can look at these things yourself and print out whatever pages you want." I walked him over, and put him into the *American Imprints* database—and *Eighteenth Century Collections Online*, too, so he could toggle into either one. A quick search of *ECCO* showed that it had the 1798 printing. I reminded him that we'd have microfilm copies for anything in either database, in case the computer images weren't good enough.

"Wow! Thanks! I was about to leave. This will save me weeks of travel and a lot of money!" As he started in, I headed back to the desk, where the Casablanca woman was waiting—and looking disappointed.

"It's not there. I tried under 'Burnett,' and double-checked under the title. It's just not there."

I sat back for a second. *That can't be right. The Pre-'56 NUC usually does pick up the ones they can't find in WorldCat.*

"I bet it *is* there."

She arched an eyebrow. *"The National Union Catalog*—the big green set? I just looked there. It's not there."

"I bet *I* could find it in the same set."

"No way. I'm sure I looked in the right places."

"I bet I can find it anyway, in the same set."

She tilted her head and raised an eyebrow, a nice little smirk on her face. "This I have to see."

We walked through the reading room, over to the door of the deck area. Her smirk never left. But then, neither did my own. *Sometimes it's good for these academics to have their assumptions set right. If you can do it at the point of use, it'll take much better than if you just mention it in a lecture. The next time, they'll be open to the possibility that they really don't know everything, and they'll seek out your help instead of assuming that what they can't find on their own can't be found at all.*

Two of the regular readers were sitting at desks over on the left. *Andrew Johnson's impeachment; and Globalization. Another one on the right—'Images of hands in Renaissance art.' The other right-side guy, French studies, not in his usual seat. I checked the clock: 3:20. Okay— his time to be down in the snack bar having tea. He's accounted for.*

The *NUC* was shelved in the first range on the other side of the Alcove door. "Wait right here," I said. "This'll just take a second." I went inside, pulled out a volume, looked for the entry 'Burnett, Murray. Everybody Comes to Rick's.' Bingo. One library location: UCLA. *This is too good.* I brought out the volume—she could see it was one of the big green books—and showed her the entry.

She stared. Her eyes widened. "No *way*! I double-checked! It wasn't there when I looked!"

I chuckled. "Well, actually, it *was* there *when* you looked; it just wasn't there *where* you looked. I should've warned you, but I thought it *would* come up in the first place. Here, come on back and I'll show you." We went into the deck area.

"The thing is, the *NUC* has two different alphabets. It goes from volume 1 with the letter 'A' to 685 with the letter 'Z.' Then at 686, right here, it starts over again with 'A', and goes to 'Z' in 754 in a completely different sequence. That happened because the whole set took so long to publish—over twenty years. After they'd already printed the early letters, citations and locations still kept coming in for parts of the alphabet they'd already published. So at the end they decided to print the late reports, too. There are 900,000 things in this second alphabet that aren't in the first one."

"But isn't this all supposed to be in WorldCat now?"

"Since nobody *put* it there, the simple answer is 'No'. OCLC, that does WorldCat, has no connection to the publisher of this set. There are thousands of entries, additional locations, and cross-references that aren't in WorldCat at all. A lot of times you can identify things through the cross-references here that give you better citations you can plug back into WorldCat—but you won't find it to begin with if you don't have a good cross-reference network. The online systems give you only keyword search capability—that can't help much when the keywords themselves have changed over the years. Sometimes the records may have a note field, but you can't count on it; and WorldCat can't display cross-references at all. The other big problem, even with the Hathi online version, is that nobody will ever scroll down 686 lines to that second alphabet on their own, without a librarian being right there to tell them about it. There's no indication on the screen that there even *is* a second alphabet."

"I'll have to tell my boyfriend about this tonight. He teaches at Georgetown. Last semester he was looking for some 1830s German book. I think he tried WorldCat and then gave up. I bet he doesn't know about this second sequence."

I bet he doesn't know about the first alphabet either. "Well, yeah. It never hurts to clue in some academic about how libraries really work." I lowered my head and raised my own eyebrow. She laughed.

"I guess not! And now *I* can read this Casablanca script—finally— right at the UCLA library when I get back. That's probably not the kind of thing I could do an interlibrary loan for. Still, it'll be worth the trip. Thanks a lot! It's funny they couldn't find it out there in their own system."

"Funny?" I thought. *Sad kind of funny. If you call the NUC a 'dinosaur' and send it to remote storage, and then tell everybody it's all in WorldCat, then you're simply guaranteed never to get any feedback that the set* does *has stuff not in WorldCat. Duhh. It's a wonder there isn't blood all over the floors of some libraries—some librarians are so good at shooting themselves and their patrons in the foot.*

"Well, the rule around here is, 'Always ask when you don't find something on your own.'"

We headed back into the reading room. "And by the way," I added, "the second rule is, 'Don't believe anybody who says you can find everything online.

The Silicon Valley Guy

I was sitting in the 6th floor cafeteria having a coffee break when a group from Assistant Librarian's office sat down a couple tables away. They didn't notice me. The A.L. and her entourage were being so deferential to a guy in a rumpled sport coat that I figured he must be some outside honcho. I remembered then that there was a lecture scheduled in fifteen minutes in the big Mumford Room, by someone from one of the big of Silicon Valley companies. This wasn't the Google guy, though, who was here last year—he, at least, seemed to think that librarians are still necessary . . . if only to help people do better Google searches. Anyway, apparently this new speaker was here "to talk and to listen to LC librarians on how to better provide the information that today's fast-paced world needs"—that, according to the flyers mounted next to the elevators in all of the buildings. Another, younger flunky shadowed him, standing back to take pictures from various angles of the group at their cafeteria conference.

A slightly rumpled blue coat, but still tailored enough to show just a hint of cuff evenly on both sides—which alone set him apart from all of the librarians he'd be talking to—and fitted blue jeans below. Not the kind you'd see on the researchers in the reading room. Ankle-high hiking boots. A Man of the People. I wondered if he'd had his shadow take his picture at the diner counter across the street—a good place to pose before actually dining at The Palm downtown. No glasses—contacts? Black knit tie—very hard to find these days, but just like Ian Fleming gave James Bond in all of the novels. The effort involved to find one nowadays suggests it's probably not a coincidence.

The Assistant Librarian, who'd been trying for years to dumb down our own online catalog to "a single search box that would seamlessly search everything" for "one-stop shopping" that would "break down silos of information" and "foster the cross-disciplinary thinking" that was needed "in today's ever-changing world"—well, she was gushing all over the guy. In fact, in previous months she'd already invited three other speakers who'd artfully rattled off the same code-speak. What all of it really meant was: We don't need standardized subject headings or cross-references to do conceptual categorization that will round up multiple variant phrasings of the same idea; all we need is a computer algorithm that will do relevance-ranking of the few guessed-at keywords the searchers type in. Offering algorithms that rank any words at all is much cheaper than providing standardized conceptual groupings of records that can be created only by human catalogers. Groupings like that bring all of the works on the same subject together, no matter what words their authors have used—in fact, no matter what languages they've written in. With standardized retrieval sets like that available, researchers don't have to specify in advance all of the right keywords for their subjects—they can just recognize whole groups of records, all under one subject heading, that they don't know how to ask for.

Beyond that, too, the managerial thinking is that we *certainly* can't keep our own cataloging in a separate "silo," with its own tailored search software, un-merged into the whole Internet. And since Internet search engines can't possibly display any cross-references or browse menus of subdivisions relating the thousands of subject headings *to each other*, well, that just means that the whole subject-headings system is no longer important. Hey, if the Internet can't handle it then it *must* be unimportant.

Another key part of the code is that libraries don't need reference librarians either, when the "disintermediation" of cross-search capabilities by that single search box enables everyone to search "everything" on their own. We no longer need to give anybody an overview of the full extent of "what the Library has"; we just need to provide them with *something* quickly. If searching "death penalty" fails to retrieve the other terms like "capital punishment" or "legal execution" or "lethal injection" or "pena de muerte" or whatever, then those records just aren't worth bothering about. Or if the algorithms searching "pro-life" and "right to choose" tunneled into completely different echo chambers, well, those word-choices probably gave the searchers the information they wanted, and isn't that what we're supposed to provide? Who needs balanced overviews? Who even *wants* them? With algorithms replacing librarians we could staff reference desks much more economically with low-level technicians; they'd only have to know how to point to where the bathrooms are, and how to "schedule appointments" with the librarians who are too important to be available for researchers at the time they actually ask for help.

Other tenets of the standard package are that we especially need "to meet students *where they are*"—even if not *when* they ask—in that "ever changing world" of ours, recognize that "scholarship is *evolving* to the Web environment," and that researchers today are all "accustomed to Google and Wikipedia." So that, of course, makes it okay if we effectively encourage them to *remain* at the level of ignorance the algorithms shunt them to, and don't bother to show them what they're missing inside real libraries, or teach them that there are better ways to see the whole shape of the literature they're after. Sophisticated algorithms can actually take the place of education itself. "Today's generation" doesn't need to know anything in advance. To be good researchers all they have to know is just how to log on and type in a few guessed-at keywords.

One advantage to believers of "the code," I always thought, is that it fits very well into a couple PowerPoint slides; the bullets make it appear that there are substantial arguments being summarized when none of them could actually be expanded beyond the level of the bullet points themselves. Besides, "nobody complains" if they just find *something* on their own. If there are a few dinosaurs who object, well, they can obviously be dismissed as just "sentimental" and "nostalgic for a card-catalog age." It's all just "resistant to change," essentially; but that gets said out loud only in closed-door meetings where none of the front-line crybabies are present.

The whole managerial litany ran through my head quickly when I saw so much of the top brass of the Library fawning over this latest Uberman from the world we're supposed to evolve into. The thought was interrupted, though, when the Man of the People heard his smartphone ring and pulled it out in the middle of the confab.

"Oh, hi—yes, everything's fine." He listened for about twenty seconds and then laughed. "Yeah, just tryin' to clean out the Augean stables. Look, I can't talk right now, but give me a call this afternoon." There was a pause. "Oh, okay, you're on her phone? Let me give you the direct number for my cell so you have it yourself." He gave the area code and then his seven digits. "The easy way to remember it is that it spells out 'TECHGUY'. Right. Talk to you later."

The library people—aka Silicon Valley groupies—waited patiently and reverently while he withdrew into his private phone world. A few minutes later, though, the group left as a whole, to get to the assembly room where his speech would be given.

I figured I'd tag along.

The Mumford Room was about three-quarters filled—a pretty good turnout for anybody. I sat towards the back door, next to Chris, one of the veteran catalogers. She, along with some of the other librarians I could see, was holding a sheet labelled "The Litany." It was a numbered list they'd drawn up after listening to all of the previous speakers who'd been invited to talk on how the Library needed to "move into the new century." It consisted of about two dozen of the required phrases I mentioned before—"evolving world," "seamless access," "cutting edge," "breaking down silos," "meeting them where they are," "catching up to the 21st century," "decoupling the strings," "one-stop shopping," "disintermediation," "disruptive technologies," "everything is now online"—the whole nine yards. Everybody was primed to keep score on how well this new guy measured up to the standards.

He was introduced by the Assistant Librarian with more of her gushes of admiration, although his background as she sketched it somehow seemed to indicate no instances of any actual contacts with real researchers. But he apparently had received much enthusiastic praise from fellow panelists at a variety of OCLC-sponsored events.

What struck me immediately was that even before he opened his mouth Chris had checked off a few of the The Litany requirements on her list: he appeared now with an open collar, no jacket and no tie— *and* he had rolled up his sleeves. She leaned over to me, whispering, "He gets extra points for rolling up his sleeves, like he's about to do some *real work*. We don't just have the plain list anymore—now everything on it is weighted according to how 'eyeball rolling inducing' it is. Talking to a Washington audience with your sleeves rolled up gets you an extra five points." I mentioned that I'd just heard him refer a few minutes earlier to "cleaning out the Augean stables"—that might count as "real work"—and wondered if that would earn him still more. She had to think about that for a couple seconds. "All by itself, no," she said. "That phrase isn't common enough to be a cliché. But if he says it in his talk I guess it *would* add to the eye-rolling impact of the sleeves. That's something the Committee would have to rule on."

As the guy started talking and droned on and I could see various librarians in the audience making checkmarks on their own copies of the list. I found out later that he had scored very well. There were a few deductions, however: while he did mention "fast-paced" and "evolving," he left out "ever-changing"; and while he did cover "seamless" and "breaking down silos" and "one stop shopping" he failed to mention "cross-disciplinary searching." Apparently, however, that caused some subsequent debate within the Committee, as to whether his use of "multidisciplinary" sufficed; but the matter was settled by the group's own rule: "No conceptual categorization is allowed; only exact keywords count for hits." "If these speakers want to live by keywords," Chris told me later, "then they get scored by them too." That seemed fair to me.

While the guy was still talking, though, I couldn't help noticing a certain air of condescension in his manner. He, flashing his Rolex watch, kept saying things like, "*You* folks are the *information professionals*; I'm here to learn from *you*." But when somebody interrupted him the first time he said it, and suggested that his company should provide an advanced search page with multiple boxes as the initial default screen, and then develop better software for word truncation, parentheses, and proximity searching that the searchers could control themselves—well, he responded that they just *couldn't* abandon their "signature" *single* search box as the default, and that some of those other things—he didn't know which ones for sure, but he said we could trust him—were already handled automatically by their black box algorithms.

He had a couple more similar interruptions from the know-nothing information professionals that went the same way; but the one everybody remembers now, in retrospect, is that he interrupted his own talk when someone's cell phone went off in the audience. *"Please,"* he said, "I'm glad to hear you have a cell phone, but we obviously need to have better control of technology right in this room!" He gave a little laugh, but the clear implication, in line with the rest of his speech, was that he was talking to a whole group who were way "behind the curve" on that front.

That didn't sit too well with me, or to the many other friends of the lady whose phone went off, so I quietly stepped out into the hall and pulled out my own phone. I dialed the area code I'd heard the guy mention in the cafeteria, then T-E-C-H-G-U-Y. I waited a few seconds out of sight; and then, as the guy's own phone went off, I heard what had to be the biggest roar of crowd laughter that had ever come out of the Mumford Room. Right after that, about three-quarters of the audience started streaming out of the room, even before the guy finished his talk. The Assistant Librarian who'd introduced him was, I'm told, visibly mortified, and didn't even try to ask for a Q & A session afterward. There weren't enough people left. Nor was the event even reported on in the next issue of *The Gazette*, the Library's internal newsletter. The guy had failed to serve The Party, so his memory was quietly erased; although I'm sure he'd continue forevermore to note on his own résumé that he'd been "Invited to speak at the Library of Congress."

I followed the crowd going down the corridor, wondering if it had ever occurred to the guy that maybe he should roll down his sleeves.

The Standard Work

From the reference desk I could hear the conversation across the room. Two young guys in the basic Congressional Intern khakis, blue sport coats and yellow ties listening to woman slightly older, mid-twenties, in a red skirt and black sweater jacket, black rimmed glasses and hair cut to her jawbone—either a TV reporter or someone higher up the pecking order in some Member's office. Those dark glasses frames showed she was *serious*, and more than just a telegenic face. From what she was saying, though, I figured 'Hill staffer.'

She looked up to the ceiling and did a great impression of an Olympic swimmer coming up for air at the end of a grueling race. Her tone was one of battled-hardened experience you might sometimes legitimately hear from someone at least twice her age. "You bet," she was saying, "I've seen a lot of bills that could've been real train wrecks. Fortunately I was in a position to change the narrative a few times, but some other cases really took down a few colleagues in the caucus; there was just nothing I could do." She sighed as though remembering, from a ship's rail, more than one suicidal man overboard. "Sometimes it's your job just to protect the Member from the incoming torpedoes shot from the same side of the aisle." *Yeah. Hill staffer—and probably the Administrative Assistant running the whole office.*

One of her bright young acolytes piped up. "That's how you got your nickname of 'Engineer Wallace', isn't it—from skirting so many train wrecks? Like that time with the pharmaceutical bill?"

The other intern nodded at the recognition of an apparently famous story. The woman herself lightly shook her head with appropriately self-deprecating modesty. "All I can say is, somebody has to be looking at all the switches ahead because the Member has too many other things to worry about. You always have to keep that in mind. In this town, you have to have more than just the whistle and the brakes; you have to have real foresight. You never know what's going to show up down the track."

Ah yes, undoubtedly sage advice on the peculiar mannerisms of the local tribe. The first acolyte piped up: "You should write a book." *Yeah, I thought. The hard fought, in-the-trenches, first-hand survivor accounts of the grueling struggles of a twenty-something former intern, now staffer, who'd helped her Congressman attach to larger bills a few riders that assured him he'd get the financial support needed from his lobbyists. Title: "Engineer Wallace: The Untold Story of a Legislative Genius." The first of a series of memoirs, I figured, with a new volume to appear every four years. National bestsellers all, ripping the cover off How Washington Really Works.*

"I probably *should* write it," she conceded. "I've been keeping a pretty detailed diary these last five years." At this strategic admission both Acolytes One and Two burst into enthusiastic nods and smiles, as though drooling for a taste of the Forbidden Fruit. At that she smiled herself, knowingly, and added, "Yes, but I'd need a good ghost writer to finesse some of the gory details." More smiles all around. "I'm not sure I could give a straight account of that time *Politico* got down on the boss for a solid three whole days, but then gave up when I got him two major TV talk-show hits the very next weekend." *Well, thank God*, I thought, *that she'd been able to administer the pure oxygen of publicity to a dying man. In DC, that counts as the ninth Corporal Work of Mercy.* "That's a story that's not even in the Wikipedia article on me."

"You have a Wikipedia article?!" number One blurted. Big mistake there. He should've not just known about it already but memorized it.

"Well, I don't approve of everything in it"—['or of your appalling *ignorance of its existence,' I figured].* "One of the previous interns wrote it all on her own a few years ago, and then got married and pregnant and moved to Minnesota. And she never updated it so I wouldn't put much stock in it." *Translation: The ingrate obviously had her priorities all wrong. Her bailing out to a white picket fence home in Never-Never land at least spared me the hassle of letting her go for lack of loyalty. If you two, however, want a recommendation after your own internship you now have the project to <u>update that article</u>.* "You don't want to draw a lot of attention to yourself, away from the boss; in this town you can be more effective if you work behind the scenes." *Translation: Ignore what I just said. A good article on me published anywhere will give me more of the clout that'll make 'The Engineer' a living legend on The Hill and get me hired in a better Member's shop.*

I must say I was having a lot of fun listening to what passes as advice in my adopted home town; but I was still at the reference desk, and just then a reader came up with a question about Alexander Hamilton. I noticed Acolyte Number Two's ears perked up immediately on overhearing the name of God's currently-chosen epitome of public attention, and I could tell he was the only one in the group straining to hear my response.

"Well, okay," I said to the reader, "have you already looked at the biography that the big Broadway show is based on?"

"Yeah," he said, "but I'd like to see what else is out there on him."

"Okay, good. I'm glad to hear somebody wants to press it more deeply. We'll have a ton of stuff on Hamilton, but a good way to start is with a biographical encyclopedia that's right around the corner. It's *American National Biography*. It's published by Oxford University Press and it's the standard work to go to for the life of any reasonably prominent American." I said that loud enough to be heard across the room. "It's particularly good not just for the quality of its articles, but for its bibliographies on the people. It'll tell you where the person's papers are and list the most important biographical sources that have already been done. In other words, it won't give you a jumble of 10,000 keyword hits—it'll steer you directly to best sources if you want to go deeper."

"That does sound like the place I want to start."

I took the guy around the corner got him into the Hamilton article.

Back at the desk, I had a few more questions about linguistic remnants of slaves' speech in Venezuelan Spanish and something about women serving as CEOs or being on corporate boards. It was a half-hour before I got reminded of the now-dispersed Congressional group.

Acolyte Number Two had hung around, though, and he came up to me with a question. "I overheard what you told another researcher a bit earlier, about there being a 'standard' biographical encyclopedia on prominent Americans. A friend of mine is curious about that, and is wondering how someone gets selected to be written up in it. Do you have to contact a particular editor at Oxford University Press?"

A friend wants to know. Sure. I wonder who that might be.

"Well, yeah," I said, "you would have to contact the publisher. But your friend would also have to meet some pretty tough criteria to get written up in that particular set."

"Oh, I don't think that would be a problem. She's sort of famous already. She's been in *Who's Who in the East* for three years now, and there's already a Wikipedia article about her."

"Well, fame at that level is certainly great and it would be necessary to get her into *American National Biography*; but she might not meet the most important qualification."

The inevitable eager question: "What's that?!" *Poor guy, I thought. He overheard me when she didn't, and probably brought to his 'friend's' attention a publicity gold mine that he happened to know about. And now he was now positioning himself to be the means of* *getting her into The Standard Work, where her fame would live forever. And maybe the success of his own internship now depended on his delivering the goods from the important 'insider's' knowledge that, in best Washington fashion, <u>he</u> alone could now bring to the table.*

"Well, there *is* one most important criterion that trumps all the other qualifications: the person written about has to be dead."

The color drained out of the poor guy's face like I'd just pushed the flush lever on a toilet. Raising the possibility of glorifying an AA and then having to retract the idea . . . well, I thought, the book that comes out of that might not be so much the on the triumphs of *Engineer Wallace* as on *The Death of a DC Intern*.

I wondered, though, if that might be enough to get the guy himself into The Standard Work.

Over the Hill

He was an old-timer in his 80s who got around pretty well with a walker. Retired from one of the local university language departments, he still came in twice a week to work on two books he was writing on French cultural history. His age was immediately apparent from his wispy gray hair and the walker; his intelligence from the fact that he kept himself on a routine to structure his days. He hadn't taught in decades but he still always wore a coat and tie, came in on the same days every week at the same time, and sat at the same desk in the reading room. I figured there must be something to such habits since he was the only 80-year-old who came in at all. He was also the only old guy I'd ever seen who'd replaced the clunky aluminum walker offered by Medicare with a different one that was collapsible, lighter, and that could be used as a cane. "It's better in cabs, too," he once told me. "I gave up driving twenty years ago, and this lets me sit in the front seat with the cabbies—they're fun to talk to—which I couldn't do with that Medicare walker. It was just too big to fit." So he gave himself things to look forward to every week, not just at the library itself, but on his rides back and forth.

He didn't have a cell phone—not even the AARP flip kind with no camera, no Internet, and no apps. In fact, he had no Internet at all—wasn't interested—and no word-processing. Out in the reading room he was always the only one writing on yellow legal pads. That didn't slow his productivity, though—he'd already published three articles, with two more in the works, on "side" discoveries he'd made while researching his books. He still used the resources that the newer people would turn up their noses at, too—he was proud, more than once, that he'd found an old book listed on a handwritten entry in the old card catalog, that never made it into the computerized version. He used old bibliographies that the younger scholars knew nothing about, and he had no problem with looking at microfilm sources—things almost entirely off-limits to the patience of the Millennials and Gen-Xers who wouldn't bother with anything old that wasn't digitized and keyword searchable on their laptops.

One of his greatest regrets was that the Librarian, twenty years ago, had eliminated stack passes for researchers who needed to browse the shelves in some areas. The old stuff he needed, especially in French, often wasn't digitized at all, and the catalog records were often minimal at best. A year ago I'd gone back and browsed the shelves myself for him, and found an 18th century historical novel there that turned out to be very useful for one of his books. Anything that old should've been in Rare Books automatically; I remembered he sighed heavily when I brought it out. "That's what I miss doing myself—I used to find things like that with some regularity. I'd make sure they went to Rare Books when I was finished with them, and there they got improved catalog records too."

All of the librarians loved the guy, as he was the embodiment of a real old-time scholar—he was way beyond any "publish or perish" considerations; he just had some ideas that he thought were important enough to pursue and to write up for others. And that's what he *did,* to keep himself going.

So I was concerned when, seeing me, he shuffled up to the desk shaking his head. Something was bothering him. "Doc," he said, "I hesitate to ask because I've already talked to the librarians in the Rare Books and the European rooms; they were very attentive but they couldn't find what I need. But I'll ask anyway because I know you keep telling me I should always ask, no matter how many other people I've talked to."

"Agreed. Let's have it."

"I need an account by Samuel Champlain of his travels in Canada, and I need the 1603 first edition. I've checked both the old card catalog and the one in Rare Books, as well as talking to the librarians. They don't have it. And they said it's not in Google Books. One of the librarians in European found a WorldCat record for copies located in some other libraries, but I doubt that any library will lend something that old. I was hoping to find a copy here but it looks like you just don't have it."

"Well, hold on—you're not done yet. Give me the title, or whatever citation you have."

He dug around in his notebook for a few seconds and came up

with it: *Des Sauvages ou Voyage de Samuel Champlain De Brouage, Fait en la France Nouvelle l'an mil six cens trois . . .* and it went on from there, probably filling up and entire octavo title page.

"Okay, let me look at that WorldCat record myself."

"That won't do me any good—the few copies listed there aren't anywhere near here."

"Granted. But it's not the library locations I'm looking for."

I pulled up the record and, sure enough, the title was listed along with a roster of far-flung libraries that own it but probably would not lend it. Farther down in the note field, however, it was also described as a microform copy having 49 images. More important, the record said it was in the "CIHM/ICMH collection de microfiches; no. 90062." I had no idea what CIHM/ICMH was, but a keyword search on that string in our own catalog snagged a Series Note attached to the title of an entire set, *Pre-1900 Canadiana: microfiche edition* having 53,000 microfiches, with a call number for the whole set in our own collection and another number for a printed guide as well. The guide was right in the reference collection; it simply confirmed the "90062" fiche number for the Champlain pamphlet. With the call number for the set, and the item number within it, the problem was solved.

"You mean you *do* have it?"

"Yeah, we do. You just have to look at it in microfiche. You can make printouts on paper if you need to—you know that already—but now you could even scan it to a flash drive if you had one." I knew he didn't; but I sometimes tried to nudge him into the 21st century. Or at least as far into it as I'd ventured myself.

"Microfiche is no problem."

"It would be for someone a quarter of your age."

"Then I'm glad I'm as old as I am. There are some advantages to being 'over the hill,' you know. I don't care if it's digitized, or paper, or carved on oak tree bark. I just want to read it."

I nodded. "This kind of thing has come up more than you'd think—last month there was a guy looking for an old serial publication from the 1880s, *Anti-Caste*. It's not in our online catalog or the old card catalog, and it's not digitized in anything covered by *Serials Solutions*, and it's not in Google Books either. But the WorldCat record for it mentions that it's in a big *Anti-Slavery* microfilm collection—we own it—and it gives the reel number. Those microform collections here are huge. Most of their books—and a lot of old journals too—are in prepackaged sets, and any one of them may have thousands of titles. The sets themselves are cataloged, but not the millions of individual items in them are not—at least, in our own catalog. But WorldCat usually provides records for all of the individual titles in most of the sets—and it'll usually identify both the set it's part of and the item number within it. Then it's just a matter of checking whether we own that collection here, and getting our own call number for it. If everything in the microform collections here were in printed formats, I think the Library would be twice the size it already is."

His smile lit up his whole face. "I'm just glad there are some librarians who can still *find* microfilms—or fiche or whatever it is. It's not just the college kids in their twenties who have the blind spots."

"Well, yeah," I said, "I think the library schools don't even mention microforms these days—they're distanced even farther away than books from all attention on the digital stuff. I'm lucky I learned about them when I was younger, but that was ages ago. I'm no Spring chicken myself. As you said, there *are* some advantages to being over the hill. When you get to be that old you can see a lot of things on the other side—stuff that the hill had just been in the way of."

The Library Ghost

I was scanning the room for some business when the guy walked past the reference desk into the reading room.

Of "India" Indian descent. Elderly, grey hair, with pens in his shirt pocket—of that generation. You don't see shirt-pocket pens in kids today. Probably an academic or an engineer. No engineer's pocket protector pouch, though; and he could be of the generation that used them. Holding a tourist map of DC in his hand. Big History Conference in town right now—go with out-of-town academic in for the confab. Wearing short-sleeve shirt and sneakers instead of leather shoes—good signals for "retired"—can dress any way that's comfortable. "Retired" consistent with his age. Prominent and shiny new watch, on a watchband that's too big for his wrist: dial face rotated off to the side of his arm. Hasn't had it adjusted: probably gift rather than purchased. No wedding ring. Who else would give an expensive watch?—could be retirement present. Consistent with his age and dress. Happy to wear it even if it doesn't fit. Maybe just got it at the historians' conference. Probably India history—would've been hired for his languages as well as background? Using the conference as an occasion to visit the Library too. Largest India collections here outside Southeast Asia. Much concern these days about Hindu nationalism in India—maybe the current hot topic?

I watched him head to the big Central Desk where readers pick up the books they've requested online. The attendant looked behind the counter and came up with about a half-dozen. That meant the guy had been here before and knew how to do the online ordering. He went over to desk 11 and sat down to look through the pile. I figured he'd be there for a while. In the meantime I checked the book catalog: "Hindu nationalism" was cross-referenced to **Hindutva** instead, as the right subject heading. 135 books there; too long a list to print for him; better: just copy the browse display mapping out the breakdown of subdivisions: specific regions, history, songs, psychological aspects, even a comic book.

With that printout done, I checked *Web of Science* and *Scopus* for literature review articles: "Hindu nationalism" or "Hindutva": a half-dozen hits, two of them each subsequently cited fifteen times. Made copies of the citations and abstracts. Checked several other database to see how many hits each would turn up on the topic: *Academic Search Complete*, 440 hits, 12 in the current year; *Public Affairs Information Service*, *Worldwide Political Science Abstracts*; *PolicyFile*, *Columbia International Affairs Online*, *Dissertations*. I was amazed that *National Technical Information Service* had thousands of relevant hits. Made sample printouts from *Academic Search* and *NTIS*. Figured I'd wait and see if they're relevant to whatever his real interest might be.

Just then he came by the reference desk, and asked the librarian across the aisle where the men's room is. *Lack of familiarity with the building layout means his previous visit was brief—long enough only to get an I.D. card, create a password and request books in the online system, then order them up for this visit, without staying at that time for an hours-long stretch.*

While he was making his pit stop I casually walked out to desk 11 to take a glancing look at the titles he was reading. Bingo: all on Hindu nationalism. I left the sample printouts on his chair.

A half hour later he came back to the reference desk, again talking to the other librarian across the aisle. "I don't know where these printouts came from but certainly they do list some interesting sources! How do I get the actual articles?"

The librarian looked at the lists and started to explain how to check for online text-versions first, and then how to look for print copies if they aren't available electronically. She finally led him back to the Computer Catalog Center across the corridor to sit down with him and show him what he needed to do. *Good for her; she didn't just point.*

I was having pretty good luck so far so I thought I'd try again: while the two of them were occupied in the other room I left another note on the guy's chair in the reading room: "Hope you're enjoying your retirement!"

Another half-hour later the guy was finished making his printouts and additional order requests at the CCC, and walked back to his desk again. Almost immediately he came back to the other librarian again, with the note in his hand.

"I just found this note at my desk—just like I found those printouts I showed you! This is most unusual." His Indian accent emphasized the "most". "I do not know where they came from! How does anyone here know that I am just retired!? My colleagues just threw me a party two nights ago! I looked around the reading room carefully and truly I did not see any of them, so who would know anything about it—or, for that matter, what project I am now working on? Did my online book orders yesterday somehow trigger extra database searches?"

The librarian could only look puzzled herself; she was as confused as he was, assuring him that nobody at the library monitors anyone's online book requests. As for the retirement note, all she could say was that maybe one of his friends was hiding in one of the many nooks out in the reading room.

"No, no. I do not think that is possible—there are not that many researchers in the reading room to begin with, and from my desk I can see everyone who comes in." He shook his head. "I have really to ask: do you have some kind of *ghost* in this library?"

The librarian shrugged her shoulders and called over to me. "Doc, you're into ghosts—did you hear what this gentleman just asked?" I nodded. "Have you ever heard of such a thing around here?"

"Well," I said, "I *am* aware of several dead bodies working in management; but I think they'd qualify more as zombies than ghosts; and in any event I doubt they'd be helpful to readers over here."

The Octopus

It was the Saturday after Thanksgiving and I was getting nostalgic for the old scheduling of the academic semesters. The reading room had about seventy people in it—not bad these days, given all of the restrictions we had that kept people out. Nowadays, readers had to be screened almost at the level of airport security—metal detectors for the people and X-ray machines for their backpacks and bags. We hadn't quite reached the level of making them take off their shoes or throw away liquids, but one of the cops—a friend of mine—told me they did turn away several people every day for having little Swiss Army pocket knives. Hey, I thought, *that's life on Capitol Hill these days*—as the T-shirt with the Capitol dome on it says, *"Toto, I don't think we're in Kansas anymore."* The next hurdle was registration for a reader card and getting their picture taken, and then mandatory cloakroom visits where their backpacks, briefcases, and purses had to be checked. By the time they had gone through all of the separate preliminary stations and made it into the reading room they were not always the happiest of campers. As for walk-in traffic, there just wasn't any left.

And then there was the Internet, too—quick look-ups for a lot of things didn't require libraries at all anymore. I had no problem with that. The problem I did have was with so many of the kids not realizing how frequently their topics required something more than *just* Internet sources. Even worse, a lot of their academic librarians told them nothing about research except "how to think critically about Web sites"—as though no other resources even existed. When the kids are taught not to even consider the possibility of library resources entirely outside the Web, well, it was no wonder traffic was down.

What really made me nostalgic, though, was the switch from the old the academic calendar. When I'd started here in the '80s, the semesters finished in January instead of before Christmas; and that put the long Thanksgiving weekend right near the point of mid-terms. That meant every kid visiting home for the weekend figured they'd use the Library of Congress while they were in town. And with no security then, no registration, no Internet, and a term-paper deadline the next week, the grand old Reading Room used to be busy at levels that seem incomprehensible today. I once counted over 300 bodies on a Thanksgiving Saturday, when there were seats for only 250.

Okay, I'm getting old. But I can still show 'em a thing or two they won't find with their laptop wireless connections. And all of the relevance-ranking, social "liking", and Web 2.0 networking in the world can't do what a librarian can, with a good collection and a little experience.

And here comes one now: an old guy—"old" means older than I am—crew cut, and in good shape—maybe military background. Short-sleeve shirt showing some kind of dragon tattoo on his left arm—Far

East connection. Probably Navy; they're more into tattoos.

He walked right up to the reference desk—no nonsense, no hesitation.

"Hello. I've got a strange request, but while I'm in town I thought I'd try what everyone tells me is the best library in the world. It's something I remember from when I was a kid, and I've been looking for it for years."

"Well," I said, "let's give it a try, whatever it is."

"I don't know even how to begin so I'll just put it all in your lap. I was a military child back in 1947. We had a set of encyclopedias and I remember a color illustration of two deep-sea divers fighting an octopus over a treasure chest. My brother also remembers pictures of the atomic bombs dropped on Japan in the same set, so the date must be around 1947-'49. Neither of us can remember the make of the encyclopedia and we've tried a lot of sources without any luck. Can you point me in the right direction on where I can find encyclopedias that old? The drawing of those divers was a real inspiration to me as a kid, and I just retired after 45 years as a professional diver. I'd just like to see it again—the picture that got me started. I'm visiting from California now, but I retired in Singapore, and the libraries there just didn't have such things."

"Okay," I said, "we may have a way to find that. Up front, though, I have to tell you we're a closed-stacks library, so you can't go back in the bookstacks and just browse around yourself. But *I* can do that."

66

Finding old illustrations is not something that can be done easily online through keyword searches; the pictures don't have searchable keywords to begin with. I'll just have to go back in our AE-class shelves, where all the old encyclopedias are grouped together, and take a look.

"This may take an hour or two for me to go back to that stacks area; can you wait that long, or can you come back later?"

"I'm only here for a few more hours—the rest of this weekend is taken up with visiting old friends for the holiday."

"Okay. That's not a problem—have a good time while you're here. If you can give me your contact information, though, either a mailing address or an email, I'll get back to you with whatever I can find; and if I don't find it exactly I can at least tell you which sources I looked in. That may narrow down future searches."

"I'd much appreciate it." He extended his right arm, and that one bore the standard Navy tattoo of an anchor with a rope coiled around it. We exchanged cards, and I told the guy to at least take a look at the magnificent Main Reading Room if he'd never been here before.

It was only that afternoon that I had a couple free hours together, to spend some time back in the stacks. And the Library did indeed have a large collection of old encyclopedias, with multiple editions from multiple years for most of them. I figured I could skip whole ranges of *Britannica*s and *Americana*s as they have distinctive bindings that people tend to remember. So I looked around the whole AE area for the lesser-known titles, especially the ones in bindings that looked old enough to date from the '40s. Each of the different titles had its different editions shelved together in chronological order, so that helped a lot.

What I found, just from flipping through volumes from many different sets, was a 1941 edition of *The Home University Encyclopedia*—it had a color illustration of two divers, a treasure chest, and a very mean octopus just as the guy had described it. I figured that the '41 date didn't make any difference, as the pre-war set undoubtedly contained many articles that were not revised in the later "1947-'49" editions—which we did not have.

I ran back to the reading room, on the off chance that the guy might still be there; but he wasn't. Still, I had his card, so that was no problem. I did have to take the book over to a friend in the Photoduplications department, because he had access to a color copier that my own division lacked. I also identified through WorldCat a couple university libraries that had a "revised" 1948 set of the same encyclopedia—undoubtedly the exact one he remembered; and I also wrote up information on Bookfinder.com and Used.addall.com if he wanted to look for old sets or volumes that might be for sale somewhere.

I mailed off everything, and about two weeks later I received a very nice response: "Outstanding! I gave this effort very little chance of success and you surprised me. What everybody told me about the Library of Congress is true—it really is the best!"

I let out a sigh upon reading that. The reason was that the Library had just announced plans to stop shelving its books by subjects, and to shelve all of them by height instead. That way you could fit many more books into the same space; and the plan was not just to use height-shelving in the offsite storage warehouses, where it made sense, but in all of the bookstacks onsite as well. And it wasn't just the new books that would be treated this way—the whole retrospective collection would be re-shelved by height, because the shelves were already full, and the new books were just piling up on the floors in the various deck areas. It was like that Mickey Mouse cartoon of "The Sorcerer's Apprentice"—the broomsticks just kept bringing in bucket after bucket of water, the march couldn't be stopped, and the chamber was drowning in the unrelenting flow. The copyright deposits were our buckets of water—they just kept coming in, unceasingly, more than a thousand new books every single day.

So, I thought, I'm glad the diver came in when he did—in a few more years his question could not have been answered at all, anywhere. He couldn't specify which encyclopedia had the illustration he wanted, so WorldCat would've been no use in locating the set; he couldn't search Google Books or Hathitrust or any other full-text database for nonverbal illustrations (even if they had *The Home University Encyclopedia*, which they didn't); and all other large libraries throughout the country had sent their own older encyclopedias out to height-shelved warehouses that couldn't be browsed. The one library in the world that always prided itself on being "the backstop" for all the others, not just because it owned more books but because it had *depth-access* to them through browsable shelving—that one library was now abandoning the shelving system that it had created to begin with, the system that allowed recognition, down to individual page levels, of information that could not be specified beforehand in full-text computer searches.

When I'd objected to the new way of shelving the books, I was of course dismissed as "sentimental" in wanting an avenue of subject access to the deep contents of old books that couldn't be duplicated online; but then the people making the decisions had never done much—or any—actual research themselves. Sometimes I'd hear, "Oh but you can browse call numbers in the online catalog"—as though searching catalog records rather than texts would work to find one particular illustration in a couple hundred yards of AE class encyclopedias.

I sighed. Was I just being nostalgic again?

No, I wasn't. With the height-shelving we weren't just throwing out the baby with the bathwater—we were tossing out whole orphanages.

The Religious Order

She came up to the reference desk and put a big expandable folder of papers on the counter. She asked me to wait a second while she sorted out her files.

The folder a thick mass of printouts and handwritten pages—more handwritten notes than usual in such a pile. Herself: short gray hair, wire-rim glasses, maybe 70 years old. Crucifix on chain around neck. Old time scholar, probably a nun from nearby Catholic University.

"Here it is," she said, pulling out one particular sheet. "I've been at Catholic University for a year, on sabbatical to work on a book, and now they're considering me for a full-time teaching position. Most of my work has been in inner-city houses working directly with people in need of social services, so I can't say I've published a lot; I think they're mainly interested in my experience rather than in publications, though. But an academic friend in Chicago said I might get more mileage out of the little I *have* published if I could say the articles have been cited by someone. She checked the list I sent her and said only one of them had been cited at all; but that was three times. And that's the article I want to turn into a book. This is the list of those three citations; I want to see if the actual articles are here."

She handed me the cites her friend sent her, but I could see in comparison with the other papers she's spread out that she'd copied them in her own regular, elegant Spenserian handwriting. *Definitely "old school"—most of the kids today don't even know what cursive handwriting is.*

"I haven't prepared a résumé in years now—no need to, what with the Order telling me where they needed me; but it seems there are academic formalities for a teaching application that I still have to observe. And apparently it 'counts' more if I can say I'm cited, or if I can quote what they say. I don't think the committee will put a lot of weight on this, but I do want my application to touch all the right bases. I'm not the only one being considered. And I would love a position in Washington—especially with access to the Library of Congress!"

"Yeah," I said, looking at the cites from *Web of Science*—the one database that all academics use to see if anyone has cited them. "We'll probably have all three of these journals. But let me take a look at our own subscription to that database—the version of it that your Chicago friend searched may not be as complete as what we have here. Libraries can pick and choose which components they want to pay for— like how deep a backfile they want—and not many libraries subscribe to the whole thing."

I did quick citation search on her article; it was something about "Practical implications of the Golden Rule," published six years ago.

"Bingo," I said. "Look at this." I turned the computer screen so she could see it directly. "It's been cited *five* times—which is pretty darn good for any humanities article these days."

"Oh, that's a surprise! Let me look . . . I didn't recognize the names of the three I had. I don't know these other two either."

"Well, that's a plus, too. Some academics—I won't say a lot—get their friends to cite them, just to inflate the count. It's usually for tenure revue. If you're being cited by people you don't even know, then it counts even more. I wouldn't put that in on your résumé, but you might mention that in the interview if they ask."

"I don't think that far ahead—I'm flattered that the University is considering me at all. I think the Order is trying to pull some strings for me. They want me to do teaching, just to pass on what I've learned, as I get into retirement age. Still, it's nice to be useful, whatever the situation—and whether I'm cited or not."

"Okay, but we're not done yet. There's another little trick here you want to use—if it works." I pointed back to the computer screen. "This side column, next to the list of those articles that cite you, has this 'Refine Results' option. Let's take a look." I clicked on the 'Web of Science Categories' link and got a new screen.

"Bingo again," I said. What this is showing is that your paper has been cited not just five times, but in five different *disciplines*—look here: the citing papers come from Religion, Philosophy, Literature, Psychology, and Sociology. You've hit the academic jackpot—you can say you've had some influence way beyond your particular subject area. Okay, it may not be earth-shaking influence in terms of numbers, but you've still pulled off the academic equivalent of drawing a straight flush. That's pretty rare—and very impressive."

"Oh, for heaven's sake! Who would've thought it?"

I made a printout of the screen for her, as well as a printout of the five article citations.

"Thank you so much! Since I *may* be staying in Washington now—we'll see how the interview goes—I'm certainly hoping to use this library much more. I'm Sister Mary Rose McLanahan." She held out her hand, her grip was surprisingly firm.

This lady is no pushover—either in a homeless shelter or, likely, in a classroom. From the way she'd pronounced 'Chicawgo' rather than "Chicahgo' I figured she's likely a native of the city—north side, anyway.

"They call me 'Doc' around here," I said, "but here's my card. It's got my email and phone number on it. But let me ask—I bet you worked at Marillac House somewhere along the line." Marillac was one of the big social services providers in Chicago—I'd volunteered there myself back in the day.

Her eyes grew as big as saucers. "How on earth—?"

I held up my hand to stop her. "Just a guess.

"But we're not finished with citing articles. Hold on a minute—I have to get something for you from my office desk."

"But you have to tell me—"

"I'll be right back."

I keep copies of a list of the dozens of databases other than *Web of Science* that enable researchers to do citation searching—finding articles that footnote any given initial source. There are about forty of 'em that even few librarians know about. I brought the printout to the reference desk.

"Here, if you have time today, take this list and look through it; it's more databases that can tell you if still other papers have footnoted your Golden Rule *magnum opus.* There are about twenty in EBSCO and as many more in ProQuest, and there's also *Scopus*, which is like *Web of Science* only a lot bigger. Your Chicago friend probably doesn't have access to these—or may not know what they can do. Show this to Jake across the corridor in the computer center—he can get you into any of them and show you what to do." Jake was a recent hire from the Catholic U. library school—he knew as much about the citation databases as I did. "Jake, by the way, just got his library degree from Catholic—maybe you've run into him out there. In any event be sure to check at least *Scopus*, *Academic Search Complete*, and *Dissertations and Theses*—they cover all subject areas across the board, sort of like *Web of Science*, but they have a lot that's not in there."

By that time there was another reader standing behind the nun, waiting to talk to me; so Sister R.M. graciously stepped aside with a "We have to talk more!" comment. She was off to the computer center.

The rest of the afternoon was pretty busy—"airport sustainability practices," "medical and health care in LBJ's Great Society," and

"Russian foreign policy in the 1700s" among the other questions. Somehow, as usual, Google and Wikipedia hadn't provided what the kids needed.

About an hour later the nun came back.

"Thank you so much for that list! I found *nine* more citing articles in those other databases! One is in an anthropology journal and two are in dissertations! I had no idea! I didn't know those databases existed!"

"Well, Sister, you're not alone there," I said.

"I have to go now, but you really have to tell me how you knew about Marillac House! I spent over fifteen years there! How on earth did you make that connection?

"Aw, shucks," I said, not without considerable exaggeration. "A guy can't give up all his secrets. But maybe I'll let you pry it out of me when you come back."

"Come back? I don't think I can stay away from this place! Just playing around with the databases on that list you gave me, I found some very good things that I think I can incorporate in my book manuscript! You'll be seeing me a lot!"

"Good. Like the joke says, 'I'm from the federal government, and I'm here to help' . . . except that the federal government itself could use a lot of help these days."

"Well, if there's anything an old nun from Chicago can do to provide it, let me know. Coffee is on me the next time I'm here!"

With that she was off.

Yeah, I thought. 'Practical implications of the Golden Rule.' Not a bad starting point for a lot of things.

*   *   *

Made in the USA
Middletown, DE
04 December 2017